# GREAT
# ARTISTS
## OF THE WORLD

### LARISSA BRANIN

SMITHMARK

*Dedication*

*To Paul, the great artist in my life*


*Acknowledgements*

*Special thanks to my parents, Dimitri and Lucille Ocasal,*
*and of course, Ann Marie Kirby.*

This edition published in 1997 by
SMITHMARK Publishers,
a division of U.S. Media Holdings, Inc.,
16 East 32nd Street, New York, NY 10016.

SMITHMARK books are available for bulk
purchase for sales promotion and premium use.
For details write or call the manager of special sales,
SMITHMARK Publishers,
16 East 32nd Street, New York, NY 10016;
(212) 532-6600.

This book was designed and produced by
Todtri Productions Limited
P.O. Box 572, New York, NY 10116-0572
FAX: (212) 279-1241


*Printed and bound in Singapore*


Library of Congress Catalog Card Number 97-066057

ISBN 0-7651-9239-X


*Author:* Larissa Branin

*Publisher:* Robert M. Tod
*Editorial Director:* Elizabeth Loonan
*Book Designer:* Mark Weinberg
*Senior Editor:* Cynthia Sternau
*Project Editor:* Ann Kirby
*Photo Editor:* Edward Douglas
*Picture Researchers:* Heather Weigel, Meiers Tambeau
*Production Coordinator:* Jay Weiser
*Desktop Associate:* Paul Kachur
*Typesetting:* Command-O Design

# Picture Credits

# CONTENTS

# FOREWORD

Art, like poetry and music, is a very personal medium. A recent visit to New York City's Museum of Modern Art presented a clear, if not amusing, example of just how much artistic tastes vary. In front of one of Jackson Pollock's famous abstract paintings, a visitor scoffed, deeming the piece "an infantile mess." Nearby—and perhaps fortunately out of earshot— another museumgoer reverently pointed out "the genius of the composition" to his equally impressed companion.

Everyone has an opinion about which artists possess greatness. Further complicating the issue are the many facets of great art—the subject, colors, and style used, and the time in which it was produced. But most of all, it is that intangible element of expressed and evoked

feeling that defines a great work of art. It is therefore not the intention of this book merely to recount *who* the great artists were, but rather to let readers determine—through viewing the accompanying works—*why* such artists as da Vinci, Rembrandt, Monet, and Picasso stood out among their peers.

In order to keep this book fairly concise, however, the number of artists and the scope of artistic periods had to be limited. This volume will recount in chronological order the lives and works of the most innovative artists throughout art history, including classical Greece, the Gothic period, Renaissance, and the Baroque era. The founders and followers of such movements as Mannerism, Romanticism, Impressionism, and Post-Impressionism will also be explored, leading to twentieth-century movements including Cubism, Fauvism, and Abstract Expressionism. As the reader will discover, each artistic period had its own effect on the next era, and every artist covered in this book broke artistic ground in some way. Most of all, it is hoped that whatever artistic preference one may have, the following pages will provide a better understanding and greater appreciation of the indelible contribution these artists made to the world of fine art.

### The Sistine Madonna

*detail; RAPHAEL, c. 1514.*
*Kunstsammlungen, Dresden.*
The two putti leaning on the balustrade in the center foreground comprise what is perhaps Raphael's most recognized image. They have since come to represent the ideal iconization of angels and cherubs in art and lore.

CHAPTER ONE

# THROUGH THE RENAISSANCE

## BEFORE THE RENNAISSANCE

The wealth of master works of art produced in pre-Christian times detail the evolution of fine art and catalog the earlier history of humankind. Many of the early works that survive today are by anonymous artists, but a number of known masters also left their marks on early art history. These artists were the masters of their day; each was influenced by the art of his time, whether it was classical or Byzantine, yet forged ahead with a unique style that later served as the foundation for the future of Western art.

## Polyclitus (Fifth Century B.C.)

Polyclitus of Argos, an innovative classical Greek sculptor, was known for his athletic statues glorifying the human form. Working primarily in bronze, he was able to move away from the static, Archaic sculptures of the past and experiment with energetic freestanding statues.

While none of Polyclitus' original works survive, his most famous statue, *Doryphorus (Spear Bearer*; c. 450–440 B.C.), has been preserved in a marble Roman copy. This famous statue depicting a man walking while holding a spear clearly conveys movement through the use of the classical Greek contrapposto position, defined by one receding, slightly bent leg. This statue so embodied the classical ideal of human beauty that it came to be known simply as the *Canon*, or measurement.

Polyclitus' work was not limited to bronze; he also worked with marble and even created a statue of the goddess Hera in ivory and gold. His work, along with many of the other great sculptors of the Greek Archaic, classical, and Hellenistic periods, inspired not only the ancient Romans but generations of sculptors and artists for centuries to come.

## Giotto di Bondone (1267–1337)

The Italian painter Giotto revolutionized Western art by moving away from the static, two-dimensional figures of Byzantine and Gothic art and rounding out the human form.

Details of his early life are hazy, but Giotto probably served as an apprentice to a local master in his native Florence. His earliest attributable and best-known work, *Virgin and Christ in the Scrovegni* (c. 1305), is a large fresco that, like all of his work, depicts a religious theme.

## Doryphorus (Spear Bearer)

*Roman copy after a bronze original c. 450–440 B.C.; by Polyclitus; marble; 6 ft. 6 in. (2 m) high. National Archaeological Museum, Naples.*
With its elegant contrapposto and detailed anatomy, *Doryphorus* so epitomized the Classical ideal of beauty that it came to be known simply as the *Canon*. Before Polyclitus, statues of free-standing nude youths, or Kouros, were extremely static.

## The Adoration of the Magi

*detail; GIOTTO, c. 1305. Scrovegni Chapel, Padua.*
Giotto emphasizes the sense of joy at Christ's birth in the spirited face of the camel. The stable boy looks up to try and contain the vivacious animal while the three kings quietly adore the Baby Jesus. Giotto's reputation for painting from nature is backed up by his attention to detail—note the realistic folds of the boy's craning neck.

## The Ognissanti Madonna

*GIOTTO, 1306–10. Tempera on wood panel;*

*10 ft. 8 in. x 6 ft. 8 in. (3.35 x 2.03 m). Uffizi Gallery, Florence.*

Painted for the Church of All Saints, or Ognissanti, the added
steps of the throne, receding canopy, and open side wings create
a three-dimensional effect. Giotto's light and dark play with
the folds in the Madonna's robe to establish a palatable form.

### The Adoration of the Magi

*GIOTTO, c. 1305; fresco.*
*Scrovegni Chapel, Padua.*
Giotto's series of forty
frescos depicting the early
life of the Virgin Mary
and the life of Christ is
considered by many to be
his greatest achievement.
These dramatic pictures
adorn the walls of the
Arena Chapel, erected
on the site of a Roman
amphitheater.

This work is distinguised by its clear break from the flat, stained-glass type figures of the past; instead, Giotto concentrates on the human form, and more importantly, human emotion.

*The Ognissanti Madonna* (1306–10) is the only panel painting indisputably rendered by his hand. Again, this work stood out due to the human, not divine, qualities bestowed upon the face of the Madonna. This approach would prove crucial to the development of Florentine painting during the Renaissance, which emphasized the human form and the contemporary world.

## Jan van Eyck (1395–1441)

Jan van Eyck helped found Ars Nova (New Arts) of fifteenth-century late Gothic painting. This style, influenced by the Renaissance occurring at the time in northern Europe, is distinguished by vivid oil colors, meticulous attention to detail, highly accurate renderings of fabrics and textures, and a definite three-dimensional effect.

It is believed van Eyck came from Limbourg. In 1422 he worked in The Hague for John of Bavaria, count of Holland. Three years later he worked for Philip the Good, duke of Burgundy, who appointed van Eyck court painter, a position he held for the rest of his life.

Van Eyck's peers were amazed by his skills with light, texture, and brilliant colors, which he enhanced by mixing linseed oil with his pigments. His portraiture is marked by a keen attention to detail, as seen in such masterpieces as *Wedding Portrait (Giovanni Arnolfini and His Wife*, 1434) and *Madonna and Child with Chancellor Rolin* (1435). It stands as a tribute to van Eyck that his Flemish brethren still referred to him as "King of Painters" as late as the sixteenth century.

**Wedding Portrait**

*detail; JAN VAN EYCK, 1434. National Gallery, London.*

Reflected in the glass is the surrounding room, decorated with ten scenes of Christ's life; a close look reveals two entering figures. The inscription above the mirror states "Jan van Eyck was here," suggesting that perhaps the artist is one of the arriving witnesses.

**Wedding Portrait**

*JAN VAN EYCK, 1434; oil on panel; 33 x 22½ in. (83.8 x 57.2 cm). National Gallery, London.*

Also known as *Giovanni Arnolfino and His Wife*, this lushly colored portrait is rich in religious symbolism. The couple soberly exchanges wedding vows while a dog—a symbol of marital fidelity—stands in the foreground. Other symbolic details include a single candle in the chandelier, representing the presence of God, as well as the couple's sandals, taken off in a gesture of respect.

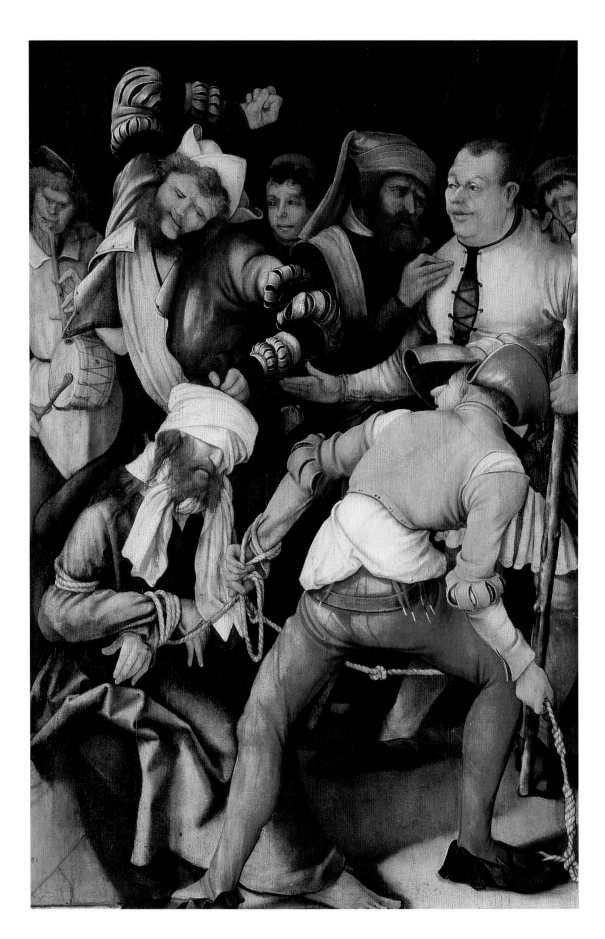

**The Mocking
of Christ**

*MATTHIAS GRÜNEWALD,
1503; oil on panel.
Alte Pinothek, Munich.*
Grünewald's brilliant
colors rivaled the
iridescent palette of
the Venetians. Here
a bloodied Christ,
in a placid blue robe,
withstands the vio-
lence of his tormen-
tors. The bright
red leggings of one
abuser and the up-
raised fist of another
brute balance the
composition and
draw the viewer's eye
to the bound Messiah.

Although his marble *David* and frescoed Adam in *Creation of Man* have come to define Michelangelo as an artist, his contributions to architecture have also stood the test of time. In 1546 Michelangelo was made chief architect of St. Peter's Basilica in Rome. Although the building was executed by Donato Bramante, it was Michelangelo who designed the exterior altar end of the building and the final form of its dome, which has since become the model for many historic buildings.

## Matthias Grünewald (1475–1528)

While the work of Matthias Grünewald (along with that of Albrecht Dürer) has come to represent the height of Renaissance influence in Germany, the artist has been more aptly described as the last of the great Gothic artists.

Born in Würzburg, Grünewald's name has long been a source of confusion, since he began incorporating his wife's surname, Niethart, in his work after their marriage in 1519. His earliest painting is the brilliantly colored and extremely vivid *Mocking of Christ* (1503), which already shows traces of the distortions and sheer emotion that dominate his later works.

His most famous work, the *Isenheim Altarpiece* (c. 1512–15), is a multipaneled altarpiece consisting of nine large panels mounted on folding wings. At the time it was produced, its intense colors were unparalleled in German art, as was the grotesque, agonizing image of Christ on the cross, which contrasted sharply with another panel's radiant image of the Messiah resurrected.

Scholars have attributed Grünewald's conceptualization to the Revelations of Saint Bridget of Sweden, a fourteenth-century mystical tome popular in Renaissance Germany. Because of Grünewald's inclination toward Protestantism, he was forced to move to Frankfurt, and then to Halle in 1527, where he died. While only ten of his paintings and about thirty-five of his drawings survive, his monumental *Isenheim* polyptych stands out as one of the final and most powerful displays of the Gothic spirit.

**The Crucifixion**

*Panel from the* Isenheim Altarpiece; *MATTHIAS GRÜNEWALD, c. 1512–15; oil on panel. Musée Unterlinden, Colmar.*
One of the three scenes from Grünewald's masterful, carved shrine. Grünewald's vivid coloring and fantastic visions bring to mind the work of the later Mannerist painters.

## Titian (c. 1480s–1576)

Considered the greatest sixteenth-century Venetian painter, Titian not only enhanced the colors and style of the painterly Venetian school, but helped shape the future of Western art.

Born Tiziano Vecellio to a family of lawyers and soldiers in the Italian Alps, Titian, like many other great artists, displayed artistic talent at a very young age and was sent to Venice to study. There he became an assistant in the studio of master painter Giorgione, and the two remained close friends until Giorgione's untimely death in 1510. Afterward, Titian altered and finished some unsold works, causing much confusion today over the authorship of many paintings, including the masterpiece *The Concert* (c. 1515).

Titian's first great solo commission was for three frescos in Padua, narratives of the *Miracles of St. Anthony* that showcased Titian's talent for rendering realistic yet larger-than-life figures. In 1516, after Giovanni Bellini's death, Titian became the official painter of the Venetian state. It was during this time that Titian began shedding Giorgione's dominant stylistic influence, adopting a style all his own. *Sacred and Profane Love* (1516) represents this turning point in Titian's career and set off a prolific period during which Titian created magnificent religious, mythological, and portrait paintings. His famous bacchanals *(Worship of Venus, Bacchanal of the Andrians*, and *Bacchus and Ariadne*; c. 1518–22), based on Roman mythology, were among the most renowned works of the Renaissance. Titian painted the figures in a classical sense, quite like Michelangelo, but went a step further by placing these ample forms in contemporary, natural settings.

Titian's paintings of the 1530s were characterized by a quietly refined color and sensuality. *Venus of Urbino* (1538–39), a revision of Giorgione's *Sleeping Venus* (1510), was Titian's best-known work and quickly became a tribute to the perfect image of feminine beauty. Again, this *Venus* is not rendered as a marble statue of the past but as a living, breathing being in a contemporary Italian palazzo.

In the years that followed, Titian produced works he himself called *poesie* ("poems"), an apt description for his poetic visions placed in mythological settings. *Danaë* (1553), *Venus and Adonis, The Rape of Europa* (c. 1550–62), all commissioned by his greatest patron, Spain's Philip II, differed from his earlier mythological works and were set in romantic, distant lands rather than contemporary palazzos.

### The Venus of Urbino

*TITIAN, 1538–39; oil on canvas; 46½ x 64¼ in. (119 x 165 cm). Uffuzi, Florence.*
This is Titian's best known image of perfect, feminine beauty.
The golden tresses of this Venus inspired Venetian women
to dip their hair in a mixture of egg shell, sulfur and orange peel,
then sun-dry it over the wide brims of crownless straw hats.

Titian's contribution to European painting was phenomenal. His legacy of loose, expressive brush not only revolutionized oil painting techniques, but provided an alternative to the Florentine tradition of painting sculpturesque, linear forms. His deft hand was subsequently celebrated by artists throughout the ages including Velázquez, Rubens, Rembrandt, and the French Impressionists.

## Raphael (1483–1520)

In his short thirty-seven years, Raphael was recognized as one of the best Italian Renaissance painters, and has since achieved fame as one of the most popular artists of all times.

Raphael (born Raffaello Santi) was the son of an Urbino painter who provided him with his early training. Raphael later studied with Timoteo Viti, and then went on to Perugia to become an assistant to the painter Perugino. Raphael emulated Perugino to such a degree that art historians have had difficulty deciphering whose hand actually rendered the paintings completed during their association.

In 1504 Raphael moved to Florence and began studying the paintings of established contemporaries such as da Vinci and Michelangelo. The impact of their work is apparent in his painting, which up until this time had been categorized as Umbrian—rigid, with an emphasis on perspective. Raphael's new works, such as *La Belle Jardinière* (1507–08), displayed a sense of da Vinci's expression and composition, while his *Entombment of Christ* (1507) featured postures and musculature inspired by Michelangelo and a composition reminiscent of Giotto.

In 1508 Raphael was commissioned by Pope Julius II to execute frescoes in four rooms of the Vatican Palace in Rome. On the walls of the first room, the *Stanza della Segnatura* (1509–11), Raphael created scenes personifying Theology, Philosophy, Poetry, and Justice. His masterpiece, *School of Athens*, on the wall beneath Philosophy, illustrates the rational search for truth and bears likenesses of himself, da Vinci, Michelangelo, and the architect Bramante.

Raphael's influence further increased after the death of Pope Julius II in 1513. With Leo X, a known humanist and patron of the arts on the pontifical throne, Raphael was made chief architect of St. Peter's Basilica in 1514. A year later, he was in charge of all the excavations of the copious antiquities in and around Rome. Even with all these extra duties, Raphael still managed to paint. His last painting, *The Transfiguration* (1517–20), was completed by one of his followers, Giulio Romano, after Raphael's untimely death.

### The Sistine Madonna

*RAPHAEL, c. 1514; oil on canvas; 8 ft. 9 in. x 6 ft. 6½ in. (2.69 x 2.01 m). Kunstsammlungen, Dresden.*
Produced during a prolific period when Raphael served both as chief architect of St. Peter's Basilica and overseer of antiquities being excavated in and around Rome, the *Sistine Madonna* was painted for Pope Julius II as his present to the city of Piazenza, Italy.

### Portrait of Perugino

*RAPHAEL, 1495–96; oil on canvas; 59 x 46 in (149.9 x 116.8 cm). Uffizi, Florence.*
This subject and author of this portrait have long been confused; at various times in history, it was thought to be a portrait of Martin Luther by Holbein, and a study of Verrocchio by Lorenzo di Credi. It wasn't until the 1930s that historians revealed its true identity, a portrait by Raphael of his mentor, the painter Perugino. The sitter's identity is confirmed by Perugino's own self-portrait.

## Pieter Bruegel the Elder (1525–1569)

For years, when he wasn't simply forgotten, Pieter Bruegel the Elder was referred to by a rather misleading nickname, "The Peasant," which no doubt arose from his many paintings of robust peasant life. However, though much about his life remains sketchy, biographers have categorically disclaimed notions that Bruegel was the voice of the people, recording such rustic scenes as a tribute to humanity. A more likely interpretation suggests that the painter's contemporaries—who enjoyed Bruegel's jolly genre scenes and regarded them as burlesques—better understood the artist's intentions than later critics who enthused over his love for mankind and deep, philosophical paintings.

### Hunters in the Snow

*PIETER BRUEGEL THE ELDER, 1565; oil on panel; 46 x 63¾ in. (116.8 x 161.9 cm). Kunsthistorisches, Vienna.*

Bruegel had an exceptional talent for evoking a mood by painting directly from observation. This atmospheric work was part of a series of paintings representing months of the year.

Conjecture aside, what is known about Bruegel is that he joined a painters' guild in 1551 and soon developed a style unlike the majority of his Flemish peers, who followed a predominantly Italian Renaissance style of painting that incorporated classically muscular nudes in mythological settings. Instead, Bruegel painted atmospheric scenes such as *Hunters in the Snow* (c. 1565) and the humorous *Peasant Dance* (1568) and *Peasant Wedding* (1568), which scholars believe may have been companion pieces. *Hunters* has since been hailed for the attention to subtle detail in the landscape, while the latter two are noted for their exceptional composition and an unblinkingly amusing eye.

## Peasant Dance

*PIETER BRUEGEL THE ELDER, 1568; oil on panel;*

*44½ x 64 in. (114 x 164 cm). Kunsthistorisches, Vienna.*

Thought to be the companion piece to Bruegel's *Peasant Wedding*, the joviality of this picture is infectious. Bruguel's eye objectively captures many scenes: cantankerous drunkards; a couple kissing; a feisty older man pulling a young peasant woman to join him in a dance; and children imitating their dancing elders.

**Descent From the Cross**

*Rosso Fiorentino, 1521; oil on panel; 11 ft. x 6 ft. 5½ in.*
*(3.35 x 1.96 m). Pinacoteca Communale, Volterra.*
The vivid colors and frozen, agitated figures in this painting broke new ground for Mannerist painting. Departing from the style of past Renaissance masters, Rosso's lamentation scene is cast in a tension-filled, angular vision.

## MANNERISM

Mannerism was a mid-sixteenth-century style of painting known for its elongated forms and crowded, almost hectic compositions. Originally a derogatory name aimed at ersatz painters imitating the great Renaissance masters, Mannerism has since become a very important and unique part of art history's prodigious timeline.

### Rosso Fiorentino (1495–1540)

Giovanni Battista di Jacopo, known as Rosso Fiorentino, was one of the leading exponents of the new Mannerist style. His dramatic masterpiece *Descent From the Cross* (1521), with its geometric, twisting figures frozen in agitated motion, was the first painting to break from the classical style of the High Renaissance.

Rosso studied with Andrea del Sarto after enrolling in the painters' guild in 1516. Although influenced by Michelangelo and Raphael, Rosso developed his own assertive style, as demonstrated in his early fresco *Assumption of the Virgin Mary* (1517), and *Madonna and Child with Saints* (1517), a painting dominated by the aggressive color red—*rosso* in Italian—which earned him his nickname.

In 1530 Rosso moved to France, where he served as court painter for King François I and helped found the famous Fountainebleau school, a term applied to all the works of art created at the residence of the French court—the château of Fontainebleau.

### Agnolo Bronzino (1503–1572)

Bronzino was an Italian painter of the Tuscan High Mannerist school, a refinement of the old Mannerist style that Bronzino defined with his coolly elegant portraits of aristocratic figures.

Born Agnolo di Cosimo, Bronzino studied with early Mannerist painter Jacopo da Pontormo, and became the court painter to the Medici family in Florence during what has been termed the elegant phase of Italian Mannerism. Although he produced several crowded Mannerist-style religious works at this time, it is his highly stylized, sedate portraits of the Medici family—such as *Cosimo de'Medici* (n.d.) and *Eleanora di Toledo with Her Son Giovanni de'Medici* (1550)—that came to define the High Mannerist style. His famously composed *Portrait of a Young Man* (c. 1535) exemplifies his approach: the man's unruffled posture, direct gaze, and limp hand epitomize a detached elegance that lend a sense of the untouchable to Florence's nobility. The composition, suffused with brilliant color and surface detail, later influenced other portrait painters, particularly the nineteenth-century French master Jean-Auguste-Dominique Ingres.

## Portrait of a Sculptor

*AGNOLO BRONZINO, n.d.;*
*oil on wood; 38½ x 30¾ in.*
*(99 x 79 cm). Louvre, Paris.*
Bronzino's portaits of
Florence's aristocracy
defined the High Mannerist
style. His style—suffused
with a sense of placid roy-
alty—attracted the wealthy
and important d'Medici
family, for whom he pro-
duced a number of portraits.

**Fray Felix Hortensio Paravicino**
*EL GRECO, c. 1605; oil on canvas; 44¹/₂ x 33³/₄ in. (113 x 85.7 cm). Museum of Fine Arts, Boston.* Here the artist pays homage to the sitter, a scholar and poet who praised El Greco's work in several sonnets. The fine craftsmanship and treatment of this portrait stems from the artist's early Venetian training.

## El Greco (1541–1614)

The last of the Mannerist painters, El Greco produced canvases rife with the elongated pale figures and supernatural, crowded spaces of Mannerist painting. Regarded as Spain's greatest religious painter, El Greco's work, along with that of Velázquez and Goya, became the pinnacle of Spanish art.

As the name El Greco ("The Greek") implies, the artist was not Spanish at all. His real name was Domenikos Theotokopoulous and he was born in Crete. His life there is not well documented, although he seems to have studied the Byzantine art popular at the time. In 1566 he moved to Venice, where he studied with the High Renaissance master Titian and admired the work of the Venetian Mannerist Tintoretto.

After moving to Rome, El Greco met several Spaniards associated with the church in Toledo who persuaded him to come to Spain to work. He arrived in Spain in 1577 and was quickly commissioned by the Church of Santo Domingo el Antiguo to paint *Assumption of the Virgin* (1577), which was influenced by the composition of Titian's *Assumption*, painted some sixty years earlier.

*The Burial of Count Orgaz* (1586) is now recognized as his greatest achievement. This towering 15 x 11 foot (4.57 x 3.36 meter) painting—still in its original place in Toledo's Church of Santo Tomé—portrays a dead Toledan nobleman being laid to rest in his grave by Saints Augustine and Stephen, as rows of identically dressed figures look on. Above these crowded, mortal figures, the count's soul rises mystically to an equally dense, swirling heaven.

Though known for these feverish, spiritual paintings and his later mythological subjects, El Greco has also been credited with painting several brooding landscapes of the city of Toledo—such as his *View of Toledo* (c. mid-1600s)—in a genre previously disregarded by Spanish artists. By the time of his death, El Greco's reputation as a great artist was solid, but not long afterward his work was deemed too personal and his reputation began to falter. It was not until the twentieth century that devotees such as Picasso brought his work once more into the spotlight.

### The Burial of Count Orgaz

*EL GRECO; 1586; oil on canvas; 16 ft. x 11 ft. 10 in. (4.9 x 3.6 m). S. Tomé, Toledo.*
This Mannerist masterpiece was inspired by the Toledan legend that upon the death of the Count of Orgaz, a noble benefactor to the church, Saints Augustine and Stephen descended from Heaven to lay the count to rest. Directly above, an angel lifts a ghostly baby (his soul) up to a birth canal-like cloud ending at the feet of Christ.

# CHAPTER TWO

# THE BAROQUE, NEOCLASSIC, AND ROMANTIC PERIODS

## THE BAROQUE

Originating in Rome and later spreading throughout Europe, the Baroque period (1600–1750) was an artistic era characterized by exuberant emotional and physical intensity, grandiose settings, and voluptuous richness. In France, the Baroque found its greatest support with the monarchy of Louis XIV. The king's extravagant palace at Versailles is a culmination of Baroque expression in architecture, painting, landscaping, sculpture, and decor that became the foundation of the short-lived, lighthearted Rococo period.

**The Martyrdom of St. Matthew**

*CARAVAGGIO, c. 1598–99; oil on canvas; 11 ft. 1 in. x 11 ft. 5 in. (3.37 x 3.48 m). Contarelli Chapel, S. Luigi dei Francesi, Rome.*
One of three scenes the artist painted from the life of Saint Matthew. Caravaggio depicted holy figures as common men, and was accused of imitating nature at the expense of ideal beauty. After the completion of the series, he devoted himself almost entirely to religious compositions and portraiture.

## Caravaggio (1573–1610)

Caravaggio, an Italian Baroque painter whose work exemplified the naturalistic style of the early seventeenth century, is often mentioned in connection with chiaroscuro (dramatic use of light and dark effects). Though he did not pioneer realism or chiaroscuro, his unique vision gave new life to these qualities.

Born Michelangelo Merisi, his moniker was derived from the Lombardy town where he was born. After apprenticeships in Milan and Rome, he began producing genre paintings featuring young men, as seen in *The Musicians* (c. 1591). His use of models from the lower classes added to the realism and simplicity that at first was criticized, especially when Carravaggio's saints were depicted with peasantlike features. This realism, however, soon gained popularity.

In 1600 Caravaggio was commissioned to decorate the Contarelli Chapel in Rome with three scenes from the life of Saint Matthew. The end result, *The Calling of Saint Matthew* (c. 1600), displays the dramatic use of light for which Carravaggio became famous. The hand gesture of Carravaggio's Christ was obviously inspired by Michelangelo's *Adam* from the Sistine Chapel ceiling.

The drama in Carravaggio's own life soon began to rival that of his works. Often imprisoned and arrested, he fled to Naples in 1606 after being charged with murder. There he painted the

**David**

*detail; GIANLORENZO BERNINI, 1623. Galleria Borghese, Rome.*
The frown of concentration and furrow in David's brow convey the sense of drama more acutely than his energetic posture.

**The Fortune Teller**

*CARAVAGGIO, 1594–95;*
*oil on canvas; 38½ x 51 in. (99 x*
*131 cm). Louvre, Paris.*
Caravaggio frequently
used models from real life.
Here, a gypsy woman
slyly slips a gold ring
from the finger of the
young, weathly man
while reading his palm.

*Flagellation of Christ* (c. 1606), which influenced the artists of that city to work with naturalism. He was later knighted in Malta, where he was again arrested on unknown charges. After escaping from a Maltese jail he went to Sicily, where he completed the monumental *Burial of Saint Lucy* (1608) and *Raising of Lazarus* (1609). Just a year later, however, he died in Tuscany after contracting a fever induced by a mistaken arrest.

Although Carravaggio discouraged potential pupils, naturalistic schools of painting soon flourished in Italy and abroad; there was even a school of Dutch painters known as the Utrecht *Caravaggisti*.

## Capture of Juliers

*PETER PAUL RUBENS, 1621; oil on canvas; Luxembourg Palace, Paris.* One of twenty-one allegorical paintings commissioned by France's dowager Queen Marie de'Medici. Rubens portrays Marie in victory, a tribute to her conquest of enemies after the assassination of her husband, King Henry IV.

## Peter Paul Rubens (1577–1640)

Considered one of the most important Flemish painters of the seventeenth century, Rubens created work that epitomizes the grand style of Baroque painting, filled with opulence, drama, movement, and vitality.

Rubens's early life could have inspired such a painting. Born in exile in what is now Germany to Calvinist parents fleeing persecutions against Protestants, his father, Jan, became the advisor and lover of Princess Anna of Saxony, wife of Prince William I of Orange. After Jan's death in 1587 the family returned to Antwerp, where they became Catholics once more. Rubens served as a court page and then decided to become a painter; he was apprenticed to three Flemish painters who were influenced by the sixteenth-century Italian Mannerist painters. By age twenty-one, Rubens was accredited the rank of master painter at the Antwerp Guild of St. Luke.

Rubens traveled to Italy, where he was employed as a painter for nine years by the duke of Mantua, and in 1605 he became the duke's emissary to King Philip III of Spain. Rubens returned to Antwerp three years later, married Isabelle Bryant, and painted their wedding picture, *The Artist and His Wife, Isabelle Bryant, in the Honeysuckle Bower*, in 1609. He became court painter to Austrian archduke Albert shortly thereafter.

His career flourished and commissions were so overwhelming that Rubens established a large workshop; he made only preliminary sketches and final touches, while apprentices did the rest. In 1621 he was commissioned to do his famous series of allegorical paintings of the Dowager Queen of France, Marie de Médici; these twenty-one canvases adorned the Luxembourg Palace in Paris. Although his beloved wife's death in 1626 left Rubens inconsolable, he remained productive as both a painter and diplomat.

His later works were marked by the happiness he found in a new wife and family, as depicted in his delightful *Garden of Love* (c. 1630s) and *Venusfest* (c. 1630–40), paintings that influenced the later Rococo masters.

### Venusfest

*PETER PAUL RUBENS,*
*c. 1630s; oil on canvas.*
*Kunsthistorisches, Vienna.*
This swirling, allegorical scene features Rubens' young wife Hèléne in the lower left hand corner, gazing directly at the viewer while being lifted up in the lustful clutches of a Satyr. Rubens' signature cherubs proliferate throughout the scene.

I·XXVII·

## Gianlorenzo Bernini (1598–1680)

Bernini was the most prolific and versatile sculptor-architect during the height of the Italian Baroque period, which was characterized by dramatic scenes and ornate, curving forms.

The son of Florentine Mannerist sculptor Pietro Bernini, Gianlorenzo was born in Naples but moved with his family to Rome in 1605, where he remained the rest of his life. A great Baroque architect and painter, Bernini has come to be known primarily as the founder of a new type of realistic sculpture, marked by a perception of immediacy and the proximity of another "invisible" object. Bernini's grimacing *David* (1623) exemplifies this style best: the biblical hero is portrayed in the very act of hurling a stone at his target, Goliath, who—although not seen by the viewer—is definitely in the statue's direct line of vision.

After completing *David*, Bernini began his first of many long commissions for St. Peter's Basilica—the huge bronze canopy for the high altar above St. Peter's tomb. In 1657 Bernini and his assistants began erecting his massive masterpiece *Throne of St. Peter* (1657–66), which was the focal point of the church. As in his earlier project *The Ecstasy of St. Theresa* (1645–52), Bernini combined his three-fold talents of sculpture, painting, and architecture to create this theatrically ornate and imaginative scene.

While working on *Throne of St. Peter*, Bernini began his last long project, the grand oval piazza in front of the basilica. The original plan was to create a complete circle framed with arcades of columns with four sets of pillars. Instead, Bernini connected the stunning colonnades with two huge walls on either side of the church's facade, likening the end result to "the embracing arms of the church."

### David

*GIANLORENZO BERNINI, 1623; marble. Galleria Borghese, Rome.*
The dynamic energy of this life-sized statue exemplifies the Baroque style in sculpture. Here, the Hebrew hero dramatically enters the space of the viewer by twisting around, readying himself to hurl the fatal rock at Goliath.

### Apollo and Daphne

*GIANLORENZO BERNINI, 1622–24; marble; 96 in. (243.8 cm) high. Galleria Borghese, Rome.*
Here, Bernini captures a dramatic moment in Greek mythology. Daphne turns into a laurel tree after praying to her father (the river god Peneus) to deliver her from the lustful clutches of Apollo, her smitten brother-in-law.

## Las Meninas

*DIEGO VELÁZQUEZ, 1656; oil on canvas; 10 ft. 5¼ in. x 9 ft.¼ in. (3.18 x 2.76 m). Prado, Madrid.* Formally titled *The Household of Philip IV, The Infanta Margarita, Accompanied by Two Maids of Honor, a Duenna and Two Dwarfs, Visits Velázquez in his studio.* Here, Velázquez captures a moment in time from the perspective of the visiting King and Queen, whose blurred features are reflected in the mirror behind their daughter, Margarita. The artist himself is immortalized in the very act of painting the Royal double portrait.

## Diego Velázquez (1599–1660)

Spain's greatest Baroque painter, Velázquez is also unquestionably one of the most outstanding artists of all time. His masterful techniques in portraiture gave life to his subjects and his individual style greatly influenced the future of European art.

A native of Seville and descended from noble Portuguese stock, Velázquez was apprenticed as a teenager to Sevillian Mannerist painter Francisco Pacheco, who subsequently became Velázquez's father-in-law. In his apprentice days, Velázquez studied contemporary Flemish and Italian realist paintings and nature.

During the course of Velázquez's career, his work fell into three categories—the *bodegón* ("kitchen piece"), portraiture, and religious scenes. Most of his work during 1617 to 1623 consisted of bodegón paintings such as *The Breakfast* (c. 1618), which was completed after his acceptance into the Guild of Saint Luke. His 1623 portrait of King Philip IV led to his employment as the king's official painter, a position he maintained the rest of his life, along with the further appointments as marshal of the royal household and planner of ceremonies. Velázquez's portraits of the homely King Philip, a product of inbreeding, were direct and realistic visions, slightly altered to emphasize the king's sovereignty.

Aside from brief, inspiring trips to Italy to study Renaissance art, Velázquez remained with King Philip's court in Madrid. Upon his return from Italy, he painted a sensitive portrait of the king's only heir, Prince Balthasar Carlos, which became quite poignant after the sickly prince's premature death. In 1660 Velázquez fulfilled his last great duty as the planner of ceremonies by taking charge of the elaborate nuptials of Maria Thérèsa of Austria to Louis XIV. Shortly thereafter, worn out from the activities and traveling, Velázquez contracted a fever and died.

Velázquez has been called a painter's painter for his extraordinary treatment of color, light, and space and his deft handling of the paintbrush. Future master painters, including Goya, Manet, Picasso, and Whistler, were heavily influenced by his work.

## Francisco Lezcano

*DIEGO VELÁZQUEZ, 1643–45; oil on canvas; 42 x 32¾ in. (106.7 x 83.2 cm). Prado, Madrid.* This moving painting depicts one of the many dwarfs who served the pleasure of King Philip IV's court. Unlike the other dandy dwarfs of the royal household, Francisco is rumpled due to a mental handicap. Velázquez' portrait is so accurate, doctors today can identify Francisco's ailment as cretinism, a congenital condition marked by a thyroid deficiency.

## Rembrandt van Rijn (1606–1669)

The myth surrounding this great Dutch artist apparently surpassed the actual events of his life. According to legend, after his well-connected wife died and his important group portrait the *Night Watch* (1642) was termed a complete failure, the artist spiraled into poverty, bankruptcy, and eventual obscurity. Modern scholars have revealed, however, that Rembrandt was sent by his parents to the Latin School. By age fourteen he was enrolled at the University of Leiden, the city of his birth, but soon left to study art with a local master. He later traveled to Amsterdam, where he studied with historical painter Pieter Lastman. Within a matter of months, Rembrandt mastered all he was taught and returned to Leiden, where, at the age of twenty-two, he began taking his own pupils.

In the 1630s Rembrandt moved to Amsterdam, where he married Saskia van Uylenburgh, the cousin of a wealthy art dealer. This led to contacts with rich patrons, who enthusiastically commissioned the young artist. With his religious and mythological works such as *The Blinding of Samson* (1636) in high demand, his studio filled with pupils. But while his professional life prospered, his personal life was marked by one misfortune after another. From 1635 to 1641 Saskia gave birth to four children. Only one son survived, and Saskia died soon after his birth. Eight years later, Rembrandt hired Hendrickje Stoffels as a housekeeper. She eventually became his common-law wife, mother of his daughter, and frequent model for many paintings, including *Woman Bathing* (1654). His opulent lifestyle soon led to bankruptcy, and his final years were marked by the death of his second wife and his only surviving son.

### The Night Watch

*REMBRANDT; 1642;*

*oil on canvas;*

*12 ft. 2 in. x 14 ft. 7 in.*

*(3.8 x 4.4 m).*

*Rijksmuseum, Amsterdam.*

Also known as *The Company of Captain Frans Banning Cocq* (who , along with Lieutenant Willem van Ruytenburch, commisioned it), this huge, Baroque canvas exemplifies the uniquely Dutch tradition of the group portrait, in which painters memorialized militia members, officers of guilds, town councils, or other institutions. Rembrandt added additional figures heighten the drama of the scene; the little blonde girl in the yellow dress was placed there more for color than dramatic effect.

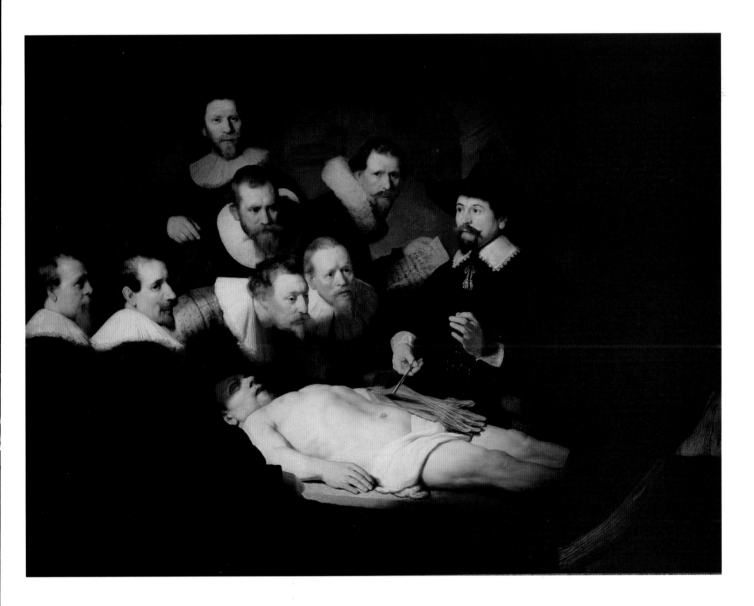

Yet Rembrandt's work never suffered from his personal tragedies—if anything, the experiences enhanced his art with an added maturity, introspection, and compassion. A chronological view of his more than sixty self-portraits offers a visual autobiography through the varied facial expressions and the dramatic light and shadow effect that have been declared Rembrandt's trademark. The staggering diversity of his work makes it difficult to choose a single piece that exemplifies his art. His masterpiece *The Night Watch*—which was actually very popular during his lifetime—epitomizes the seventeenth-century Dutch Baroque style with its crowded, dramatic setting, while *The Anatomy Lesson of Dr. Tulp* (1632) captures a theme common among Dutch artists. Both paintings broke the rules of group portraiture by realistically portraying patrons in dramatic, nonstatic poses.

One of Rembrandt's last paintings, the *Return of the Prodigal Son* (1669), depicts a stirring scene celebrating the Christian ideal of forgiveness. Always a religious man, Rembrandt's final somber biblical themes focused mainly on humanity and man's submission to God's will, a tenet in which Rembrandt, with all his misfortunes in life, seemed well-versed.

### The Anatomy Lesson of Dr. Tulp

*REMBRANDT, 1632; oil on canvas; 6 ft. 6 1/4 x 7 ft. 2 3/4 in. (1.70 x 2.17 m). Mauritshuis, The Hague.*

While the subject matter may seem grotesque, painting the anatomy lessons of the surgeon's guild of Amsterdam was a trend among seventeenth century Dutch artists; tickets were sometimes sold for public dissections.

# Jan Vermeer (1632–1675)

**The Lacemaker**

*JAN VERMEER, c. 1665;*
*oil on canvas; 9½ x 8 in.*
*(24.1 x 20.3 cm).*
*Louvre, Paris.*
This small painting
presents all the quali-
ties that distinguish
Vermeer's work: a
serene study of a
woman engaged in
an everyday task,
a harmonious blue
and yellow chromatic
scale, and most of
all, a sense of immedi-
acy. Signed "I Meer"
to the right of the
woman's head, this
piece was bought
for the collection of
Napoleon II in 1870.

Often called the great realist for the magnificent sense of naturalism in his paintings, the Dutch artist Vermeer also perfected composition and light in his many canvases featuring geometrically balanced interior settings cloaked in a golden, atmospheric light. These interiors often portray stylish Dutch gentry as they play musical instruments, talk, or quietly read or sew.

Little is known about Vermeer's personal life except what can be traced from his native city's archives. From these centuries-old records biographers have determined that Vermeer was born in Delft, began a six-year apprenticeship under a Dutch painter, and was admitted to the guild of Saint Luke of Delft as a master painter in 1653. That same year, he married Catharina Bolnes, with whom he had eight children. By 1662 Vermeer was elected governor of the Guild, a position he retained throughout four terms.

Although items left behind in his estate imply he lived comfortably, Vermeer struggled the many years of his short life and left his widow in debt. His financial plight was due in part to the Reformation; when Holland threw off Catholic rule, a major source of traditional patronage was gone, leaving artists to sell their wares at open-air booths, quite reminiscent to today's flea markets.

Vermeer may have supplemented his income as an art dealer, but war with France caused an economic slump and Vermeer was often forced to part with great works of art from which he had hoped to make a profit, receiving instead very paltry sums. Today, only thirty-five of Vermeer's own canvases survive. Other paintings have been attributed to the artist, but with some plausibility.

Further complicating his legacy is the fact that during World War II—by which time it was deemed priceless—Vermeer's work was forged and sold to the Germans. Vermeer's work had fallen into obscurity after his death but was rediscovered in the late nineteenth century by the French art critic Thoré-Bürger, who published an article on his work

**The Girl with a Pearl Earring**

*JAN VERMEER, c. 1665; oil on canvas;*
*18¼ x 15¾ in. (46.4 x 40 cm).*
*Mauritshuis, The Hague.*
An exquisite example of Vermeer's
mastery of light, shadow and
color; although there is a prop-
less background, this exotically
dressed young woman inhabits
her own three-dimensional space.
One can almost sense the subtle
movement of her veil and detect that
she has just wet her lips to speak.

in the *Gazette des Beaux-Arts*. More articles were to follow, each heralding Vermeer's paintings and instigating a new interest in this mysterious, "forgotten" genius whom Thoré-Bürger dubbed the "Sphinx of Delft."

Vermeer's serene studies of light and his harmony of colors recently reentered the public consciousness and broadened appreciation for his art. In 1996 national exhibits of his paintings drew new admirers and received the same rave reviews Vermeer's work garnered during his "rediscovery" period in 1866. Each revival affirms Vermeer as one of the foremost masters of composition and space, and beyond doubt, as one of the great realists.

## William Hogarth (1697–1764)

William Hogarth made his mark by creating a new type of picture: the morality play. His dramatic pictures and engravings focused on the darker side of human nature. Prints such as *The Orgy* from *The Rake's Progress* (1735) were rife with symbolism and social commentary. Such dramatic narratives were very popular with the masses and were never viewed as prudish or heavy-handed. Hogarth himself described his work as "modern moral subjects, similar to

**The Painter and His Pug**

*WILLIAM HOGARTH, 1745;*

*oil on canvas. Tate Gallery, London.*

Over the years, there has been much conjecture about Hogarth. Here the artist depicts himself as a seemingly innocuous sort, yet the biting sarcasm and downright wrath displayed in his work—which made him one of the earliest and perhaps most potent political cartoonists—betray him to a degree.

representations on the stage." His parables particularly appealed to the growing middle-class of tradesman, artisans, and shopkeepers, described by historian Derek Jarret as "a nation openly proud of their virtues and secretly fascinated by their vices."

Born in London, Hogarth was no stranger to the poverty and disgrace portrayed in his work. After his father's business failed, the entire family was imprisoned for five years due to unpaid debt. This exposure to desperate hardship—not to mention Hogarth's Presbyterian background, which upheld the belief that art should provide a moral purpose—led to work that incorporated both a scathing realism and a profound moralist theme.

Hogarth was also the first artist to gain a public following in the modern sense. The popularity he experienced during his lifetime may have been heightened by his anti-Methodist engravings, which reflected the beliefs of many in his society. His engraving *Credulity, Superstition and Fanaticism* (1762) linked the purported enthusiasm of the religion to sexual excitement and madness. In this engraving, a preacher taunts the congregation with puppets of a witch and devil, while another clergyman lustily grasps a woman. In effect, Hogarth an artist turned social critic. Other engravings of this nature include *A Harlot's Progress* (1732), which chronicles the moral corruption of a country girl gone bad in London. *Marriage à la Mode* (1745) is a satirical exposé chronicling the disintegration of an aristocratic marriage. Hogarth is also known today for founding St. Martin's Lane, the most prominent art academy in London before the Royal Academy.

## The Contract

*Scene from* Marriage à la Mode *series;*
*WILLIAM HOGARTH, 1745; oil on canvas.*
*National Gallery, London.*
In this satirical painting, which was also reproduced in a popular series of prints, a young aristocratic couple enter an arranged marriage and are insidiously bound like the shackled dogs (symbols of marital fidelity) at their feet. As lawyers eagerly go over their assets and prepare the marital contract, the bride woefully twists her handkerchief while her frilly, future groom turns his head in boredom.

## Mrs. Siddons

*THOMAS GAINSBOROUGH,*
*1785; oil on canvas;*
*49¹/₂ x 39 in. (125.7 x 99 cm).*
*National Gallery, London.*
Sarah Siddons was the
leading actress of the
Drury Lane Theatre.
Contrary to rival
portrait painter
Sir Joshua Reynolds,
who portrayed Siddons
as the tragic muse,
Gainsborough shows
Siddons in her contem-
porary street clothes.

# Canaletto (1697–1768)

Canaletto (born Giovanni Antonio Canal)
was the most famous Venetian view painter
of the eighteenth century. His paintings of
Venetian architecture are famous for their
accuracy, composition, and most notably,
the artist's meticulous attention to detail
and natural light.

Canaletto started out painting theater
scenery, a trade inherited from his father.
But after a 1719 trip to Rome, Canaletto
became inspired by topography. He was
soon painting views of Venice, distinguished
by strong contrasts of light and shadow. Like
many other artists, including Vermeer,
Canaletto was known to refine his compositions through use of the camera obscura,
a box that projected an image elsewhere
(albeit upside down) for viewing. His work
focused mainly on Venetian scenery, but
increasing numbers of English patrons
encouraged him to expand his repertoire by
including subjects from Rome and the
Venetian mainland. It may have also been on
behalf of his patrons abroad that Canaletto
used graphic arts such as etchings and pen-
and-ink drawings, which could be reproduced more easily than paintings.

In 1746 Canaletto moved to England,
where his views of London architecture and
country homes were very popular. In time,
however, his work became mannered and
mechanical, reaching such a point that
rumors began circulating that finished

## London: Westminster Abbey with a Procession of the Knights of the Order of the Bath

*CANALETTO, 1749; oil on canvas; 38¹/₂ x 39¹/₂ in.*
*(99 x 101.5 cm). Westminster Abbey, London.*
Canaletto received numerous commissions during his stay in England,
including this portrayal of a ceremonial
procession. Less evident here than is
his Venetian marketplace paintings is
Canaletto's desire to capture everyday
life, but the work clearly expresses an
English sense of pageantry and loyalty.

**Mr. and Mrs. Andrews**

*THOMAS GAINSBOROUGH,*
*1748; oil on canvas;*
*27½ x 47 in. (69.9 x 119.4 cm).*
*National Gallery, London.*
One of Gainsborough's
earlier paintings, this
double portrait of an
English country squire
and his new bride can
just as easily serve as a
portrait of Andrews's ex-
pansive farmland. The
harmonious blending of
the two results in a lyricism
that made Gainsborough
the most popular portrait
painter of his time.

works were in fact done by an impostor. Canaletto returned to Venice in 1755 and continued to paint there until his death. His style of painting was very influential in Italy and abroad.

## Thomas Gainsborough (1727–1788)

Thomas Gainsborough was one of the greatest British masters of eighteenth-century portraiture and landscapes. His portraits are characterized by the graceful poses of nobility, while his landscapes depict a sentimental harmony between man and nature.

Gainsborough was born in Suffolk, some fifty miles northeast of London into a middle-class family of clothing manufacturers. Displaying a talent for painting at an early age, Gainsborough began to study with a silver engraver at age thirteen and later studied with historical painter Francis Haymon. Gainsborough's early work *John Plampin* (c. 1750s), clearly influenced by French Rococo painter Antoine Watteau, duplicates the pose Watteau himself used for an aristocrat's portrait. One of Gainsborough's most famous portraits during this time, *Mr. and Mrs. Andrews* (c. 1748), is unique in its balance of portrait and landscape, as well as its cool, crisp lines.

From 1760 to 1774 Gainsborough lived and painted in Bath, the fashionable health resort immortalized in the novels of Jane Austen. During this time he was also elected one of the first members of the Royal Academy of Arts and was commissioned to paint the portraits of King George III and the Queen consort, Charlotte Sophia. In 1774 he returned to London, where he became the most popular painter of the British aristocracy. Works from this period include the famous *Mrs. Siddons* (1785) and *The Blue Boy* (1779).

Although he was making his fortune portraying London gentry in their finest silks and plumes, Gainsborough felt a kinship with the more humble lower classes, which he depicted in beautiful landscapes, as in *Girl with Pigs* (1782). This style fell in line with the new, late eighteenth-century spirit that praised the virtues of the common people. These heartfelt genre paintings were enthusiastically admired by the wealthy London society, who ironically paid high prices for these portrayals of poverty.

By the time of his death Gainsborough was widely admired, especially by his former rival, the great portrait painter Sir Joshua Reynolds. At Gainsborough's funeral, Reynolds, president of the Royal Academy, acknowledged Gainsborough as "one of the greatest ornaments of our Academy."

*FOLLOWING PAGE:*
**Piazza San Marco:**
**Looking toward**
**San Geminiano**

*CANALETTO, n.d.;*
*oil on canvas; 26¾ x 36½ in.*
*(68.5 x 93.5 cm).*
*National Gallery, Rome.*
Canaletto's mastery of
painting architecture
and light leave the
viewer with an extra-
ordinary sense of
having just entered the
painting, feeling the
warmth of the mid-day
sun and the breeze that
rustles the awnings.

**Man Painting
a Woman**

*KITAGAWA UTAMARO, n.d.;
print. Musée Guimet, Paris.*
Utamaro's focus on facial
expression, as well as
his use of color and
contour heavily influ-
enced Western art. His
method of rendering fig-
ures through color alone
was later emulated by the
French Impressionists.

**Sunrise, With a Boat Between Headlands**

*JOSEPH MALLORD WILLIAM TURNER, 1835–40; oil on canvas; 36 x 48¼ in. (91.4 x 122.6 cm). Tate Gallery, London.* Pre-dating Impressionism, works like this were hesitantly received in Turner's own day: After his death, many such paintings were disregarded as unfinished. They were discovered years later, rolled up in the dank cellars of the National Gallery in London, where they were once mistaken as an old tarpaulin.

While studying in the studio of Katsukawa Shunsho in 1775, Hokusai discovered the new technique of woodcut printmaking, which was becoming very popular. For fifteen years he created a staggering number of book illustrations and color prints inspired by traditional tales and by the ordinary lives of the Japanese. After Shunsho's death, Hokusai left the studio and began studying works ranging from that of his own countrymen (such as Kano) to the Dutch engravings he was exposed to through a single trade port in Nagasaki.

Hokusai's careful study of works from the West inspired his later works, such as the famous blockprint series Thirty-Six Views of Mount Fuji (1825–33). These authentically painted yet stylized prints, such as *Red Fuji* (1825), departed from the Japanese tradition of portraying characters from the Kabuki theater. Instead, Hokusai broke new ground by painting landscapes from a lower perspective, which he adopted from the Dutch works he studied. This East-meets-West phenomenon was reversed a century later when Hokusai's prints were discovered and became the rage of the Parisian art scene.

## Joseph Mallord William Turner (1775–1851)

Viewing Turner's atmospheric paintings, it is easy to comprehend how this English painter's dynamic studies of natural light and color on both land and sea led to the development of Impressionism.

Born in London, Turner studied at the Royal Academy of Arts, where he first exhibited his work at age fifteen. Over the years he was elected to several positions within the esteemed academy, becoming an associate in 1799, then a full member three years later. In 1807 he was the academy's professor of perspective and in 1845 was appointed deputy professor.

While Turner's early works were mostly watercolors, by the late 1790s he began exhibiting his first oil paintings. His later works have fallen into three categories. The first, a twenty-year period starting in 1800, is characterized by detailed, picturesque historical and mythological settings, with a palette restrained to earth tones. From 1820 to 1835, however, Turner's paint became more vibrant and his views blurry. *Ulysses Deriding Polyphemus* (1829) best illustrates this phase in his career and foreshadows his ability to evoke emotion through the use of light and brilliant color.

In his final period (1835–45), Turner achieved the brilliance for which he is recognized today. Imaginative paintings during this time—usually depicting forces of nature, such as *Snow Storm: Steam Boat off a Harbor's Mouth* (1842)—were composed of indistinct forms that, through Turner's luminous colors and shimmering light, created not just a scene but a powerful aura.

**Buttermere Lake, With Part of Cromack Water, Cumberland: A Shower.**

*JOSEPH MALLORD WILLIAM TURNER, 1798; oil on canvas; 36 x 48 in. (91.8 x 121.9 cm). Tate Gallery, London.*

Upon exhibition, Turner submitted the following as an interpretation: "Till in the Western Sky the downward sun looks out effulgent–the rapid radiance instananeous strikes / The illumin'd mountains–in a yellow mist / Bestriding earth–the grand ethereal bow / Shoots up immense, and every hue unfolds."

—*The Seasons*, a poem by JAMES THOMPSON

# Ando Hiroshige (1797–1858)

Hiroshige was a Japanese painter and print-maker known as the last of the great *ukiyo-e* (everyday scenes) figures in printmaking. Inspired as a youth by Hokusai, the founder of ukiyo-e, Hiroshige perfected the structure of Hokusai's innovative landscapes by incorporating his own sense of lyricism.

The son of a fire brigade chief, Hiroshige entered the studio of Utagawa Toyoshiro. After his master's death he turned toward landscape painting, influenced by the ground-breaking paintings of Mount Fuji created by Hokusai.

Hiroshige's peak of success and genius can be measured by his 1833 masterpiece, Fifty-three Stations of the Tokaido, a print series depicting scenes on the highway connecting Edo and Kyoto. This series not only displayed Hiroshige's strong sense of color and skilled variations on the changing seasons, it also enabled Hiroshige to challenge the supremacy of his mentor and rival, Hokusai.

With this success, Hiroshige gained great popularity, especially for the poetic visions he interjected into his landscapes, which imbued a Japanese sense of balance and harmony. Hiroshige continued making prints for other travel series, including *One Hundred Famous Views of Edo* (1857), as well as bird and flower compositions. Toward the end of his career he published a large work with three landscapes containing the essentials of Japanese scenery—snow, flowers, and the moon. By the time of his death, Hiroshige was already regarded, along with Hokusai, as one of the dominant forces in nineteenth-century Japanese art.

## Kanazawa Temple

*ANDO HIROSHIGE, 1857; woodcut.*
*Private Collection of Pierre Bonnard, France.*
The subdued monochrome hues and lyrical charm of Hiroshige's woodcuts, shown at the Paris Expo, greatly influenced such nineteenth century artists such as van Gogh, Whistler, and Cassatt, who began experimenting in the medium.

## "Oko Uwanare Uchi Nozo"

*Right wing of a triptych; ANDO HIROSHIGE, n.d.;*
*woodcut. Private Collection of Edouard Vuillard, France.*
Hiroshige often portrayed everyday people doing everyday chores; this woodcut depicts a traditional rite. Unlike past works, Hiroshige's revelers have individual personality—the various positions of their arms and the twisting of their bodies give the picture a sense of candor and movement.

## Eugene Delacroix (1798–1863)

Delacroix is classified by scholars as the greatest painter of the French Romantic movement, a school characterized by its sweeping, dramatic scenes. His subtle treatment of color was also influential in the future development of Impressionist and Post-Impressionist painters.

Born toward the end of the Rococo period, Delacroix began taking art lessons as a teenager. In 1822 the young painter submitted his first picture, *Dante and Virgil in Hell*, to the Paris Salon exhibition. His next Salon entry, which the French government purchased, was the emotionally charged *Massacre at Chios* (1824), recording an event on the Greek island of Chios in which twenty thousand Greeks were killed by Turks.

In the same vein, Delacroix painted his most famous work, *The 28th July: Liberty Leading the People* (1831), inspired by a five-day French uprising reminiscent of the French Revolution almost forty years before. While most of his works during this time were inspired by historical battle themes, many others were derived from his lifelong love of literature, such as his painting for the 1827 Salon, *The Death of Sardanapalus* (1827), based on a Lord Byron poem.

Delacroix found further inspiration during a trip to England, where he visited the galleries and the theater. Of particular interest to him were the paintings of John Constable,

### Dante and Virgil in Hell

*EUGENE DELACROIX, 1822; oil on canvas; 6 ft. 2¾ in. x 7 ft. 10 in. (1.89 x 2.41 m). Louvre, Paris.* Alternatively titled *The Bark of Dante, Dante and Virgil in Hell* was Delacroix's first Paris Salon triumph. Inspired by Dante's *Inferno*, the red-robed figure is the Latin poet Virgil, who guides Dante through Hell as the writhing, demonic souls of immoral Florentines struggle to get into the boat. Such dramatic and exotic literary scenes became very popular during the Romantic movement.

## Pierre-Auguste Renoir (1841–1919)

"Why shouldn't art be pretty?" Renoir famously declared, "There are enough unpleasant things in the world." This sentiment perhaps best describes the widespread attraction to his work. His favorite subjects—beautiful children, tranquil landscapes filled with flowers, and most of all, feminine women—are among the most beloved of all the Impressionist painters.

Born in Limoges, France, Renoir began working as a painter in a porcelain factory, which perhaps inspired the use of the fresh, airy colors seen throughout his career. As a young artist, Renoir was greatly influenced by the happy settings of the great Rococo masters, which he studied intently at the Louvre.

After making the acquaintance of other painters, including Claude Monet in 1862, Renoir became one of the leading members of the Impressionist group. Like his fellow Impressionists, Renoir struggled with hardship until he met the art dealer Paul Durand-Ruel, who championed the controversial works of the Impressionists and purchased many of their works.

By 1881, however, Renoir was feeling a bit stifled by the Impressionist label. He visited Italy, where his work became a bit somber and more solid, portraying mythological themes as in his *Judgment of Paris* (1913–14). Renoir mockingly called this period of his career "the sour manner." In his later years his arthritic condition led to confinement in a wheelchair, though he continued to paint and sculpt until his death.

### The Swing

*PIERRE-AUGUSTE RENOIR, 1876; oil on canvas;*
*35¼ x 28¾ (92 x 73 cm). Musée d'Orsay, Paris.*

This carefree scene took place in the garden of Renoir's home in Montmartre. Like his fellow Impressionists, Renoir concentrated on the light effects of the sun, which play off the grass, and are soaked up gloriously by the woman's white dress.

### Dance in The Country

*PIERRE-AUGUSTE RENOIR, 1885; oil on canvas;*
*71 x 35½ in. (180 x 90 cm). Musée d'Orsay, Paris.*

This joyful scene features one of Renoir's favorite models, Suzanne, a popular sitter for many artists at the time, including Toulousse-Lautrec. This painting is a good example of Renoir's use of women, color and flowers in creating what he liked to call "beautiful" paintings.

# Mary Cassatt (1844–1926)

The American-born painter Mary Cassatt spent the majority of her life living and working in France. Primarily self-taught, she eventually became a member of the Impressionist group, Société des Artistes Indépendants.

### Child in His Mother's Arms

*MARY CASSATT, c. 1890; pastel; 31½ x 25¼ in. (81 x 65 cm). Pushkin Museum of Fine Arts, Russia.* Touching displays of maternal affection became a recurrent theme in Cassatt's paintings, but she approached them in a diverse number of media. Here, Cassatt uses pastels, influenced by her friend and mentor Edgar Degas; later, inspired by Japanese woodcuts, Cassatt would experiment with drypoint.

Born in Allegheny City (now Pittsburgh), Pennsylvania, Cassatt began studying art in 1861 at the Pennsylvania Academy of Fine Arts in Philadelphia. Her family apparently considered her interest in art as a whim—during Victorian times, the notion of a woman choosing a career in art was not only unconventional, it was downright scandalous. Not surprisingly, Cassatt's final decision to become an artist met with her family's violent disapproval. Even more disconcerting to the elder Cassatts was their daughter's plan to go off to Europe and study art by viewing works of the Old Masters. Ultimately, Cassatt's father relented only after it was agreed that Mrs. Cassatt would accompany Mary and make sure she was properly set up in Paris.

After a brief enrollment in the workshop of an academic painter, Cassatt abandoned his tutelage in favor of independent study at various museums, including the Louvre and the Ecole des Beaux-Arts. There she meticulously studied and copied the works of the seventeenth-century realists she admired, especially Frans Hals. The influence of Old Masters such as Rubens and Velázquez is quite evident in Cassatt's early works, such as *The Musical Party* (1874) and *The Mandolin Player* (1868), her first piece accepted by the Paris Salon.

Intensely interested in contemporary art, Cassatt soon began incorporating Impressionism into her paintings. Influenced as she was by the soft pastels of Degas, it was a breakthrough for her when he noticed one of her paintings at the Salon and asked her to join the Independents. Although her long friendship with Degas—whom she considered a mentor—was sometimes marred by his penchant for caustic remarks, it was nevertheless a relationship built on a mutual, unequivocal devotion to art.

Disliking the necessity of painting on commission, Cassatt instead used household help and family members as models, particularly her sister Lydia. In utilizing these familiar figures, Cassatt created tranquil, domestic settings, focusing particularly on tender mother-and-child themes, as depicted in *The Bath* (1891). It is this milieu that has endured as Cassatt's trademark.

Cassatt was always striving to learn more about her craft. In 1890 she was awed by a major exhibition of Japanese art, which had a pronounced influence on late nineteenth-century French art. The unique spatial qualities, careful lines, and delicate colors of Japanese woodcuts became a source of inspiration for many Impressionists, including Cassatt. At the age of forty-six, Cassatt had her first solo show, which displayed her re-creations of the domestic scenes of her oil paintings, masterfully executed with the graphic technique *intaglio* (Italian for "to cut").

Although Cassatt enjoyed artistic accolades in France (she received the Légion d'honneur in 1904), she was not widely received in her own country until after 1912, whereupon her alma mater, the Pennsylvania Academy of Art, awarded her a Gold Medal of Honor.

### Young Woman Sewing in a Garden

*MARY CASSATT, 1886; oil on canvas; 36 x 25½ in. (91.4 x 64.8 cm). Jeu de Paume Museum, Paris.* Cassatt often captured quiet, domestic moments such as this. Here Cassatt paints the background with deft, Impressionist strokes yet lends her own more exacting style to the form of the girl—a cross between contemporary art and the portraiture of the masters she so greatly admired.

## POST-IMPRESSIONISM

Although *Post-Impressionism* may seem a rather bland term to describe the highly innovative artwork that immediately followed Impressionism, the lack of a more descriptive word in no way lessons the importance of this period. During this time artists utilized the various influences of the past and forged ahead with their own unique styles; in the process they laid the groundwork for twentieth-century art.

## Paul Cézanne (1839–1906)

Often referred to as the father of modern painting, Cézanne's bold, colorful studies of still lifes and landscapes inspired the daring Cubist and Fauvist movements of early twentieth-century art.

Born in southern France's Aix-en-Provence, Cézanne was the only son of a self-made financier. At private school in Aix, Cézanne met future novelist Emile Zola, who became a close friend. At the insistence of his domineering father, Cézanne studied law from 1859 to 1861, though he continued attending drawing classes. His final decision to meet Zola in Paris and become a painter caused much friction with his father, who wanted him to become a banker.

But Cézanne had other plans. Given to violent tempers and depression, he talked his father into submitting to his wishes. In 1861 he joined Zola in Paris and attended the Atelier Suisse, beginning a lifelong habit of visiting the Louvre to study and sketch the works of the masters. Another habit formed at this time was the recurrence of fits of rage and self-doubt over his artistry. It reached such a point that Zola, as quoted in Angus Wilson's *Emile Zola*, privately opined, "Paul may have the genius of a great painter, but he never will have the genius to become one. The least obstacle makes him despair."

Soon Cézanne became acquainted with the Impressionists, with whom he would exhibit works in 1874 and 1877, but he remained outside their tight circle and after being repeatedly rejected by the Salon, he became a

### Still Life with Fruit Basket

*PAUL CÉZANNE, c. 1888–90; oil on canvas;*
*25¹/₂ x 32 in. (65 x 81 cm). Musée d'Orsay, Paris.*
Beautiful harmony and balance of his still life paintings typify Cézanne's meticulous attention to the form and color of all his subjects. Each strategically placed element is captured in full detail, yet is integrated into the overall scene.

While Klimt's paintings featuring sloe-eyed femme fatales, such as *Judith I* (1901), came to symbolize the dangerous side of sexual attraction, his famous painting *The Kiss* (1907–8), is a luminous ode to erotic love. Other admired works include his series of Mosaic Murals (1905–9) in the Palais Stoclet, an extravagant, private mansion in Brussels designed by Josef Hoffmann, a fellow member of the Vienna Secession movement.

Klimt's originality was a culmination of artistic sources, ranging from of classical Greek, Byzantine, and late-medieval artwork, to the woodcuts of Albrecht Dürer and the symbolic art of Max Klinger. Today, Klimt's decadent paintings represent one of the more imaginative artistic ways of combining naturalism and symbolism.

**The Scream**

*EDVARD MUNCH, 1893;*
*tempera and pastels on cardboard;*
*35½ x 28½ in. (91 x 73.5 cm).*
*National Gallery, Oslo.*

An ominous sea and sky seem to be swallowing the screaming, androgynous figure, while the bridge and a silhouetted couple remain unfazed by the maddening swirl; the contrast adds depth and a sense of urgency to the scene.

## Henri Toulouse-Lautrec (1864–1901)

Toulouse-Lautrec's lively paintings and posters of Paris nightlife exuberantly captured the vibrancy of the colorful scene of which he was very much a part. His keen sense of color and spatial technique used in his later lithographs also greatly enhanced the medium.

Born into a rich family (his father was descended from the semiroyal counts of Toulouse), he was a very sickly child, and his future was altered after he broke both legs, in two separate accidents. The bones never healed properly and eventually stopped growing, leaving Lautrec deformed in adulthood, with a normal-sized torso and abnormally shortened legs—he stood a mere four and a half feet tall. Daunted by his image, Lautrec threw himself into art, became a heavy drinker, and compensated for his appearance with an engaging personality.

Having studied academic art in Paris, Toulouse-Lautrec came into his own as an artist during his nocturnal visits to both the fashionable nightclubs of Montmartre and the brothels of Paris. In both settings, Lautrec deftly captured mood and gesture with his quick charcoal sketches, which he later taped to his studio walls as reference for larger paintings, such as his famous *At the Moulin Rouge* (1892).

In the late 1890s Lautrec's excessive drinking began to catch up with him and his work began to deteriorate. By 1899 the artist suffered a complete mental breakdown and was confined to a sanitarium for a time; he suffered a second breakdown and died at the age of thirty-seven. His work is celebrated not just for its bon vivance, but for its historic value as an accurate documentation of his generation.

**In the Salon at the Rue des Moulins**

*HENRI DE TOULOUSSE-LAUTREC, 1894; charcoal and oil on canvas; 43½ x 51½ in. (111.5 x 132.5 cm). Musée Toulouse-Lautrec, Albi.* The artist was very familiar with the interior of this particular brothel, producing many sketches and paintings of the prostitutes there. The rich color scheme successfully evokes a sense of decadence.

### Singer Yvette Guilbert Taking a Curtain Call

*Henri de Toulousse-Lautrec, 1894; oil on photographic enlargement of a lithograph; 18³/₄ x 9³/₄ in. (48 x 25 cm). Musée Toulouse-Lautrec, Albi.*

The popular singer of at the Moulin Rouge often complained of Lautrec's unflattering portraits of her (he did many), which she called distorted. Lautrec did not idealize his subjects: instead, he openly displayed the subject's inner life, whether good or bad.

# CHAPTER FOUR

# TWENTIETH-CENTURY ART

Twentieth-century art comprises a staggering number of artistic movements (or "isms"), some occurring successively, others simultaneously. The century began boldly with a vibrant movement called Fauvism, followed by the equally startling Cubist style. Other movements included nonobjective painting, Surrealism, Abstract Expressionism, and Pop Art. The modern artists presented here represent the various movements that have marked this century, and have illuminated the artistic path toward the next millennium.

## Wassily Kandinsky (1866–1944)

Kandinsky was one of the first founders of nonobjective, pure abstract paintings. The artist also led the influential Munich group Der Blaue Reiter (The Blue Rider; 1911–14), which held several avant-garde exhibitions featuring abstract paintings characterized by their vibrant colors and organic forms.

Like fellow Bauhaus faculty teacher Paul Klee, Kandinsky was an accomplished musician from Moscow and incorporated music into his paintings, even claiming he heard music when he saw color. Works in this vein include *Sketch I for Composition VII* (1913). In 1886 Kandinsky enrolled at the University of Moscow, where he studied law. Nine years later, he attended his first French Impressionist show, resulting in a move to Munich to receive a basic art education, which in those days included life drawing and anatomy.

Soon after his formal training in the rudiments of art Kandinsky was freely applying paint to canvases with the bold brushwork and vibrant colors inspired by Fauvism. Unlike the Fauves, however, Kandinsky did not seek to represent recognizable subjects. Instead, his aim was to stir a spiritual meaning through his use of forms and colors.

By 1903 Kandinsky's work was known all over Europe and, of course, initially met with public criticism. His work reached the United States through several exhibits and the fervent support of Solomon Guggenheim of New York's Guggenheim Museum.

## Henri Matisse (1869–1954)

Hailed as the most important French artist of the twentieth century, Matisse, like his great rival Pablo Picasso, covered much ground during his long and varied career. Matisse's name, however, is inextricably linked to Fauvism, the innovative movement that he led. The term

**Harmony in Red**

*Henri Matisse, 1908–09; oil on canvas; 69³⁄4 x 86 in. (177.1 x 218.4 cm). Hermitage, St. Petersburg.*
This masterpiec)e is painted over two of Matisse's earlier works. The first, entitled
*Harmony in Green*, explains the landscape outside the window; the second, *Harmony in
Blue*, was purchased, but Matisse convinced the owner (a collector of his work) to let him
re-work the painting on last time. Fortunately for the art world, the owner acquiesced.

**Composition VI**

*WASSILLY KANDINSKY,*
*1913; oil on canvas;*
*6 ft. 3 ³/4 in. x 9 ft. 6 ³/4 in.*
*(1.94 x 2.94 m).*
*Hermitage, St. Petersburg.*
Though he was inspired
by the Fauves, Kandinsky
did not depict recog-
nizable forms in his
work, instead striving
to stir spiritual meaning
through bold use of col-
ors and abstract forms.

**Dance (II)**

*HENRI MATISSE,*
*1909–10; oil on canvas;*
*9 ft. 5½ in. x 12 ft 9 in.*
*(260 x 391 cm).*
*Hermitage, St. Petersburg.*
These exuberant figures
were originally found in
the background of Matisse's
*Joy of Life (1906)* and are
based on the artist's memory
of Catalan fisherman doing a
round dance, called *sardana*.
The dancers also conjure
up images of The Three
Graces, the mythological
figures found in the Med-
ieval and Renaissance art.

*Fauvism* (from the French *les fauves*, "wild beasts"), was first used by an art critic to describe the group's boldly colored canvases; although the term stuck, Matisse's work and nature were far from uninhibited. The artist was in fact very methodical and intellectual in both his painting and his personality.

Born in a small village in northern France, Matisse was the son of a grain merchant and did not show an interest in art until he began painting while recovering from appendicitus. He later commented that from that moment on, he did not lead his life, it led him. Very soon after his illness, he became a full-time art student in Paris and began copying works of the masters at the Louvre.

During this time in his early career Matisse discovered the works of the Impressionists and Pointillists. The influence of these free-spirited, rebellious movements led Matisse to give up the idea of becoming a copyist. Instead he founded his own, radical approach to color by utilizing bold areas of flat, pure color. This new way of painting inevitably caused a public outcry, and Fauvism was born.

By the early twentieth century, however, the movement ended and Matisse was not to be associated with a particular school again. Matisse detested such concepts of association, be-lieving that artists should not be labeled or trapped by their own reputations. The style by which he is most often recognized is best exemplified in his *Harmony in Red* (1908–9) and *Joy of Life* (1905–6). Diagnosed with cancer in 1941, Matisse was eventually confined to a wheelchair, but his condition did not stop this prolific artist. In his eighties, Matisse completed the magnificent interiors and stained glass windows of the Chapel of the Rosary in Vence, located on the French Riviera.

## Paul Klee (1880–1940)

Mischievous, magical, and mysterious: these are the words that biographers and admirers alike most often use in describing the inspired works of Paul Klee, a Swiss-born German Expressionist painter, known for his whimsical paintings and works of graphic art.

Born into a musical family, Klee himself was a talented violinist who wrestled with the decision to study art over music before enrolling at the Munich Academy in 1900. Klee's early artistic influences included his teacher, the popular society painter Franz von Stuck, as well as Goya and the early Christian and Byzantine art he discovered while touring Italy in 1901. While in Italy Klee also admired the works of da Vinci, the Sistine Chapel, and particularly Botticelli's *Birth of Venus*, which he considered "the most accomplished painting."

Klee's paintings, watercolors, and etchings are hard to categorize neatly; they combine elements Surrealism and Cubism with primitive and children's art. Klee once remarked that critics likened his work to the naive scribbles of children, but instead of taking umbrage at such comments, the artist revealingly exclaimed, "If only it were true!"

In 1906 Klee became acquainted with Munich's avant-garde art circles and for the first time displayed his pen and ink etchings, the best known of which were his earlier works *Each Believing the Other to Be of Higher Rank* and *Two Men Meet* (1903). During this time Klee struck up a significant friendship with painter Wassily Kandinsky, who urged Klee to join his cutting-edge Expressionist group Der Blaue Reiter, which was highly influential in the development of pure, abstract art.

An inspiring trip to Tunisia led Klee to begin experimenting with color and light. He later created entire compositions comprised of shimmering colored squares such as *Hammamet with Mosque* (1914) and *Southern Tunisian Gardens* (1919), which resembled the mosaics he had encountered.

After World War I, both Klee and Kandinsky were teachers at the influential Bauhaus school, where Kandinsky was to write several essays on art theory, including *Pedagogical Sketchbook* (1925). Klee began teaching at Düsseldorf Academy in the early thirties, but was fired by the Nazis, who labeled his work "degenerate." He fled to Switzerland in 1933, where his later works were distinguished by thick black lines and forms resembling primitive art, as rendered in *Embrace* (1939) and *Rock Flora* (1940).

### Jardin de Chateau

*PAUL KLEE, 1919; oil on canvas. Basel, Kunsthalle.*

Inspired by the colorful mosaics the artist encountered during a trip to Tunisia, this patchwork, almost quilt-like painting conveys the bewitching bright, white heat of the area.

## Pablo Picasso (1881–1973)

In the nine decades of his life, Picasso was probably the most prolific and versatile artist of all time and definitely one of the most inspired artists of the twentieth century.

Born in Malaga, on the southern coast of Spain, Picasso was the son of an art instructor. Biographers have long recorded that Picasso could draw before he could speak, and his father, Don José, began giving him serious art lessons at age seven. Legend has it that by age thirteen Picasso's talent so surpassed his father's that the latter handed his brushes and palette to his son, vowing to never paint again.

After Picasso's mature, realistic drawing of a nude model stunned the examination jury at Barcelona's School of Fine Arts (where his father taught), he was promptly enrolled. When his son won an honorable mention at the National Exhibition of Fine Arts in Madrid, Don José decided it was time for his prodigy to attend the best art school in Spain—the Royal Academy of San Fernando in Madrid.

While he may have had good intentions, Picasso's restless energy and fierce independence made it impossible for him to attend class and he stopped going soon after enrollment. He returned to Barcelona in 1899 and became a popular regular of the Bohemian set, which met nightly at a local tavern called Els Quatre Gats ("The Four Cats"). Constantly creating art, Picasso soon had his own show at Els Quatre Gats and received good press. Once again the artist grew restless, and he moved on to Paris. There he quickly began to experiment with the techniques of others, most notably Van Gogh, Gauguin, Renoir, and Toulouse-Lautrec, who clearly influenced his *Le Moulin de la Galette* (1900).

Picasso's introduction to the prominent art dealer Ambroise Vollard led to his first, critically acclaimed show in Paris. While the reviews were exuberant, critic Félicien Fagus observed, "Picasso's passionate surge forward has not yet left him the leisure to forge for himself a personal style."

Soon after this show Picasso entered what has since been dubbed his Blue Period. His blue-tinged canvases were often stark and melancholy, featuring beggars and prostitutes. The elongated forms emphasized poverty and malnourishment, but also served as a tribute to El Greco, whom Picasso greatly admired. During this time, paintings such as *The Old Guitarist* (1903) brought him his first commercial success, as did the later, warmer paintings completed during his Rose Period. These tender paintings often featured elements of circus life, complete with harlequins and circus animals.

Always restless with the familiar, Picasso soon ventured toward the unknown and came up with a painting that shook the art world's solid foundation, in effect altering the course of Western art. That painting, *Les Demoiselles d'Avignon* (c. 1906), was the seed from which Cubism was born. At the time, however, the controversial painting—which broke every artistic, aesthetic rule—was greatly ridiculed. The young French painter Georges Braque at first derailed the painting too, but soon joined forces with Picasso, becoming Cubism's cofounder.

Picasso went on to break new ground by inventing the medium of collage in his *Still Life with Chair Caning* (1912). While other artists followed suit and remained in the mediums he founded, Picasso was insatiable, constantly working in different styles and mediums, striving to reach new, unexplored artistic levels. During the mid-thirties, as the bloody civil wars in Spain raged on, Picasso's work became increasingly violent. Turning to his canvas to vent his disgust over the bombing of a little town in northern Spain, Picasso created *Guernica* (1937), the greatest antiwar statement in fine art.

The later years of Picasso's career were extremely productive. Already a successful painter, Picasso explored sculpture, printmaking, and ceramics, often rendering stunning creations from everyday items and junk. Predominant themes included his life-long devotion to bullfighting,

**Portrait of Ambrose Vollard**

*1909–10; oil on canvas;*

*36 x 25½ in. (91.4 x 64.8 cm).*

*Pushkin Museum, Moscow.*

Completed just four years after his breakthrough *Les Demoiselles d'Avignon*, this prism-like portrait of the famous Parisan art dealer epitomized Picasso's fully matured Cubist style.

### Les Demoiselles d'Avignon

*PABLO PICASSO, 1906; oil on canvas; 96 x 92 in. (243.9 x233.7 cm). The Museum of Modern Art, New York.*
Considered by many to be the beginning of Cubism, at the time it was pro-
duced *Les Demoiselles d'Avignon* sparked laughter and ridicule—one art critic
wrote that Picasso would be found hanging in front of the painting someday.
Needless to say, the painting was banished to a dark corner of Picasso's
studio, where it remained a for good many years before being displayed again.

and re-creating works of the masters. This time, however, he copied artists like El Greco and Velázquez, using his own unique style.

By 1967 paintings from his Blue Period sold for over $500,000—a staggering amount at that time for the work of a living artist. Nowadays a Picasso fetches millions of dollars. By the time of his death in 1973, the intense, black-eyed Spaniard was already hailed as the most successful artist of the twentieth century and that sentiment still stands today.

## Edward Hopper (1882–1956)

Hopper's direct studies of American life, particularly that of the lonely, gained national fame: they seemed accessible to everyone, and are still widely reproduced today. The clean lines of Hopper's American landscapes and especially his New York cityscapes display a painstakingly observed reality, and expression of the stark solitude that often prevails against the bustling backdrop of a metropolitan city or picturesque countryside.

Born in Nyack, a small riverside town about twenty miles north of Manhattan, Hopper expressed a desire to paint early, but his hardworking parents encouraged their son to attend New York City's Correspondence School of Illustrating. A year into his enrollment, however, Hopper transferred to the Chase School, or New York School of Art, where he studied with Robert Henri.

After a European excursion, Hopper hit financially hard times and reluctantly supported himself as a commercial illustrator. Throughout those years, however, he still managed to show his works at various exhibitions, producing etchings and watercolors, and became quite successful. Soon he was known as one of the leading interpreters of American Scene painting, expressing the loneliness of big-city life.

*Nighthawks* (1942), Hopper's most famous and often-duplicated painting, depicts an austere late-night diner. The street outside is empty, the expressions of the diners, minimal, and as with most Hopper works, there is little interaction between the subjects. The images such as those in *Nighthawks*, *New York Movie* (1939), and *Sunlight in a Cafeteria* (1958) justified Hopper's

**Nighthawks**
*EDWARD HOPPER, 1942;*
*oil on canvas; 33¼ x 60 in.*
*(84.5 x 152.4 cm).*
*Art Institute of Chicago.*
One of art history's
most recognizable scenes.
Here Hopper reveals
his voyeuristic tendencies
and masterful lighting
abilities. Typical of his
works, the interaction
in the scene is minimal.

growing reputation as the artist who instilled a visual definition of isolation and city-life boredom. While many art historians have claimed Hopper's work bore psychological imprints, the artist himself disliked confirming such statements, instead declaring that his goal was to just paint what he saw.

### Amedeo Modigliani (1884–1920)

During his short career, Italian painter and sculptor Modigliani developed a style completely unparalleled. His lush, provocative nudes and deft portrait studies are recognized by their elegant, elongated forms.

Born in Italy, Modigliani settled in 1906 in Paris, a city teeming with artistic genius. Here he was influenced by Toulouse-Lautrec and his colorful studies of Parisian nightlife; by Picasso, who was in his Blue Period; and most of all, by Cézanne. Modigliani emulated Cézanne's still-life technique in his portrait paintings, often creating backgrounds consisting of large panels of color. Like Cézanne, he utilized variations in color and texture to give the canvas a rich vibrancy.

Modigliani's friendship with Romanian sculptor Constantin Brancusi helped foster his highly mannered style. Brancusi introduced the painter to primitive African sculpture, which soon became a passion and heavily influenced his portraits. The elongated faces; almond-shaped eyes, sometimes hollowed out; and tiny, pursed lips all stem from Modigliani's fascination with African masks.

Unfortunately, his personal life was plagued with poverty, ill health, and excessive alcohol and drug intake. Tuberculosis claimed his life at the age of thirty-five, and, like many other great artists, he died in relative obscurity.

**Hotel Room**

*EDWARD HOPPER, 1931; oil on canvas; 60 x 65 in. (152.4 x 165.1 cm). Museo Thyssen-Bornemisza, Madrid.* Hopper often painted scenes in hotel rooms. The models are usually in repose, as here. The viewer is left to discern the contents of the letter in the woman's hand, and given her candid, dejected pose, one can only give in to an active imagination.

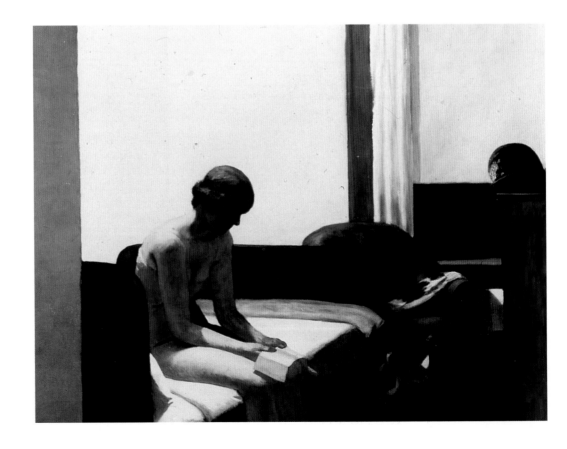

### The Yellow Sweater

*AMEDEO MODIGLIANI,*
*1918–19; oil on canvas.*
*Guggenheim, New York.*
One of Modigliani's
many portraits of his
wife, Jeanne Hébuterne.
While the features are
not highly stylized, there
is a strong sense of the
woman's quiet, melan-
choly nature. Two days
after Modigliani's pre-
mature death, Jeanne—
nine months pregnant—
jumped from a five story
window to her death.

### Diego Rivera (1886–1957)

Known as a Mexican muralist painter, Rivera captured some of history's most significant moments, not just those of Mexico, but of humankind. His rounded yet solid figures, often of farmers and laborers, adorn the walls of many public buildings throughout Mexico and the United States.

Rivera was born in Guanajuato, Mexico, and later moved to Mexico City, studying at the San Carlos Academy and the carving workshop of José Guadalupe Posada. In 1907 Rivera received a four-year scholarship for European study and promptly began studying in Spain with realist Eduardo Chicharro. Within two years, Rivera traveled to Paris, where he continued his studies

**Dream of a Summer Night**

*MARC CHAGALL; n.d.; oil on canvas. Musée des Beaux-Arts, Genoble.* This whimsical, dream-like scene exemplifies Chagall's seemingly unconscious method of painting. The unreality and magical qualities of his work highly influenced the Surrealists.

Throughout the sixties, Warhol used silk-screen ink and polymer paint on canvas to reproduce pop culture icons, including popular comic-strip characters, Campbell's soup cans, Coca-Cola bottles, and movie stars. Warhol's trendy, aluminum-foil-wallpapered studio, the Factory, became the hip meeting place for New York's avant-garde art scene. Here he worked on his silk screens and on the short underground films he produced and directed, which have since attained cult status. In 1968 Valerie Solanis (founder and sole member of the Society for Cutting Up Men, or S.C.U.M.) shot Warhol at the Factory, nearly killing him, and inspiring the 1996 independent film *I Shot Andy Warhol*, which faithfully recreates the look and feel of this period in Warhol's life.

Warhol continued producing and exhibiting an astonishing amount of work during the 1970s, including his famous *Mao* paintings (1972–74). The silver-wigged artist also became known for holding court at the ultra-chic, sybaritic Studio 54 nightclub in New York City with his famous entourage of friends, including Liza Minelli, Mick and Bianca Jagger, Liz Taylor, and Truman Capote, who became subjects of his now-famous portraits.

By the 1980s Warhol was already a legend. He continued exhibiting his work all over the world and collaborated for a few years with the ill-fated graffiti artist Jean-Michel Basquiat. After Warhol's own untimely death during gall bladder surgery in 1987, he was eulogized as "having held the most revealing mirror up to his generation."

## Two Hundred Campbell's Soup Cans

*ANDY WARHOL, 1962; synthetic polymer paint and silkscreen ink on canvas; 6 ft. x 8 ft. 4 in. (1.82 x 2.54 m). The Andy Warhol Foundation for the Visual Arts/ARS, New York.*
Warhol broke new ground by taking ordinary and familiar items, such as Campbell soup cans and brillo pad boxes, and turning them into works of art. Like most works in this medium, Warhol used the image over and over in different ways.

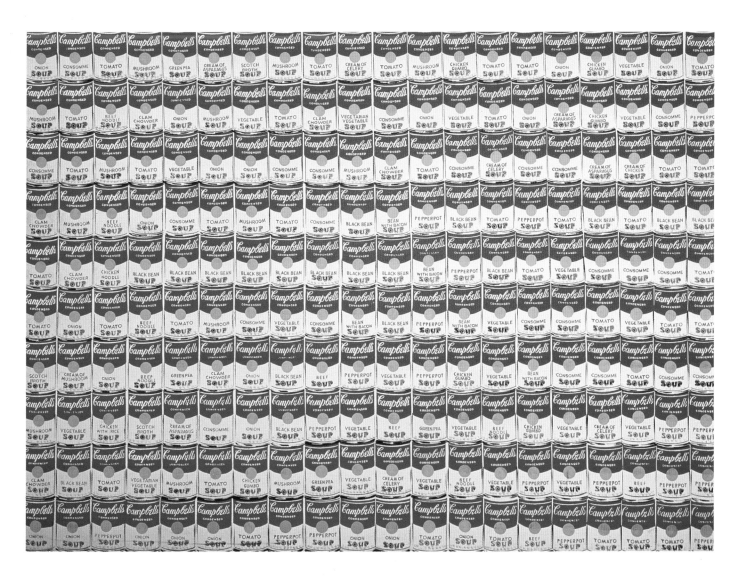

Page numbers in **boldface** type indicate photo captions.